SALES
ON A SNAPSHOT

ROBERTO CASTANGIA
MATTIA CASSANELLI

SNAPROGRAMME
Smart. Short. Simple.

SUMMARY

5   - How to get the most out of this book
6   - Introduction
7   - The SNAProgramme
8   - The book series
10 - To whom it is addressed
11 - About this book
12 - About the authors

13 - SALES A: Sales on a snapshot
15 - Create a need for your product
17 - Find prospects
19 - Make the phone your best friend
21 - Qualify the prospects
23 - Sell the solution
25 - Follow up
27 - Negotiate!
29 - Close the deal
31 - Support your customer

33 - SALES B: Pre-sales - From opportunity generation to meeting
35 - Trust your product
37 - Spot new opportunities
39 - Actively build opportunities
41 - Passively build opportunities
43 - Build a relationship
45 - Prepare your meetings
47 - Ask for budget constraints (BANT)
49 - Understand the authority (BANT)
51 - Understand the need (BANT)
53 - Ask for timelines (BANT)

55 - SALES C: Pre-sales - From meeting to deal
57 - Master your communication
59 - Build the case
61 - Hold the hand!
63 - Tailor your proposal
65 - Chase!
67 - Close the deal

69 - SALES D: Post sales - Building the trust
71 - Support your customers
73 - Treat your customers as your best friend
75 - Chase your money
77 - Ask for referrals
79 - Ask for feedback
81 - Be proactive and minimise complaints
83 - If disruptions occur, manage them!

85 - SALES E: Handling complaints
87 - Evaluate complaint
89 - Respond promptly
91 - Offer options for resolution with timelines
93 - Be ready to accept the cost
95 - Ask for feedback!
97 - Set preventive actions for the future

99 - SALES F: Repeat Business (Get the most out of your current clients)
101 -   Know your customer
103 -   Assess values and needs
105 -   Keep in touch
107 - Plan for the next proposal
109 - Develop new opportunities

111 - SALES G: Business Etiquette
113 - Create a network
115 - Dress to impress!
117 - Get ready for the meeting
119 - Look after your customers

121 - SALES H: Targets
123 - Anticipate risks and success
125 - Track your progress
127 - Deliver!

HOW TO GET THE MOST OUT OF THIS BOOK

This book is divided into sections that cover the content. For each section, there are summaries called snapshots, which outline the most important concepts.

When completing each section, make sure you go back to its snapshot. Below you have the steps to read this book. These steps will be the same whether you are a child, student, or professional. You can use the same steps as a guideline whether you are a parent who reads this book for your child or if you are a coach who wants to encourage thinking.

1. First, visualise the image
2. Read the title of the image.
3. Close your eyes and recreate the image in your mind
4. Focus on details, from objects to colours, to the character's position, and to possible sounds they could be making. Make sure you involve all of the senses.
5. Move to the black-and-white image.
6. Read the story that is in the orange box and focus on the words in bold.
7. Focus on the bolded key points, which are connected to the black-and-white image.
8. Make the image live and recreate the story in your mind.
9. When your mind can visualise the full image, move to the next one.

The SNAProgramme is based on memorisation techniques. Memorisation is key! Only funny, grotesque, disproportionate, painful, scary, or disgusting events, will stick to your long-term memory. Unleash your memorisation and enjoy your reading!

Introduction

There is currently a great deal of value in learning scientific, humanistic and linguistic subjects in all age groups. However, there is evidence of a structurally sufficient capacity in the systematic learning of interpersonal and behavioural skills. Unlike the so-called "hard skills", which in relation to individual technical skills, soft skills are attributes that are more pertinent to personality traits, that is, skills related to the emotional intelligence of the individuals and the society in which they live, that inform how people learn, think, and act,

Recent research carried out in the field 1-4*, demonstrates how structured educational programmes aimed to improve soft skills, have benefits on the emotional and relational stability of the students, promoting optimism and self-efficacy for the success in the future. Moreover, it is believed that within five years one third of the skills will be linked to skills that are now still considered marginal.

It is therefore of fundamental importance to make the learning of relational and behavioural skills accessible with a simple, intuitive and fast method, so that the person's training can be completed both on a personal and professional level.

*REFERENCES

1. Lyu, Wenjing & Liu, Jin. (2021). Soft skills, hard skills: What matters most? Evidence from job postings. Applied Energy. 300. 117307. 10.1016/j.apenergy.2021.117307.
2. Cegolon, Andrea. (2023). Soft skills and general education. 23. 112-122. 10.36253/form-13757.
3. Bholane, Kishor. (2022). Soft Skills for Today's Business World
4. Heckman, James & Kautz, Tim. (2012). Hard Evidence on Soft Skills. Labour economics. 19. 451-464. 10.1016/j.labeco.2012.05.014

SNAPROGRAMME
Smart. Short. Simple.

The SNAProgramme

The SNAProgramme - acronym of Soft-skills Neurolinguistic Advanced Programme - is an innovative learning method that combines neurolinguistic communication with memory techniques.
Here the focus turns words to images, making the learning process easier, faster, and the long lasting.

The SNAProgramme was developed by Dr Roberto Castangia and by Dr Mattia Cassanelli as a result of an extensive academic and commercial experience acquired by training and from developing dozens of professional teams. In a finger's "snap", SNAProgramme simplifies complex concepts for people of all ages and professions, without resorting to complex textbooks or expensive courses difficult to complete in today's busy lives of professionals, students, and children.

The SNAProgramme stands out for its simple and engaging visual style. The use of images in this program is reminiscent of charming cartoons that attract children's imagination. This deliberate choice aims to awaken the inner curiosity and creativity that resides within each individual, regardless of age or profession. By incorporating this playful element, the SNAProgramme fosters a sense of enjoyment and exploration, making the learning experience enjoyable. The use of relatable and visually appealing images helps to simplify complex concepts, enabling participants to grasp information more easily as well as retain the informationfor longer periods of time. This approach not only enhances the learning process but also encourages individuals to embrace their innate love for discovery, ensuring that education becomes a source of inspiration and lifelong growth.

The Book Series

This series of instructional books relies on the SNAProgramme to make accessible concepts about soft-skills that are not usually covered in textbooks or university modules, and commonly developed in the late phase of professional careers.

Hundreds of books have been written to describe these topics under the intention to drive the reader through the writer's experience. However, these approaches often led to dilution of the critical information and compromise in conciseness, leaving behind "the What?" and "the How?" (Should I do) of the practicality.

The SNAProgramme covers the topics as processes and describes each phase in a step-by-step basis, providing only the critical points distilled into three to four main "actions".

Whilst characters and colours are specific to each book, different scenes identify each step for an easy memorisation process. Each book is then divided into sections covering each a subject in separate illustrations.

Simple stories accompany each step to expand the importance of the concepts, making the point accessible to adults as well as children. In fact, SNAProgramme enables for the first time to share the learning process across different generations.

The series is divided in books and they cover:

1. Sales (Products and Services)
2. Negotiation
3. Communication and public speaking
4. Time management
5. Project Management
6. Problem solving
7. Marketing
8. Leadership
9. Team Management
10. Persuasion
11. Money management and financial independence
12. Work / life balance
13. Memory
14. Scientific Method
15. Work ethics and emotional intelligence

To whom it is addressed

The programme is aimed for people of all ages and professions, including professionals, students and children.

Professionals: the SNAProgramme reinforces the concepts acquired during the work experience and proposes them in a more intuitive and easily memorable perspective. The goal is to consolidate the concepts already known to the professionals, see these concepts from another perspective and have a complete understanding of the professional knowledge by learning new concepts and techniques in the areas of relational and behavioural skills.

Students: the SNAProgramme helps students complete their training during the years of study, otherwise mainly focused on learning technical skills.

Children: the SNAProgramme allows children to learn concepts, such as emotional stability and personal growth in a fun way. The goal is to give awareness as well as mastery of soft skills in everyday life, so that children can cultivate a highly competitive way of reasoning during youth. This would be the first series of books in literature that allow simultaneous learning of soft skills for children and parents.

About this book (SALES)

Dear reader, this book will present you the Sales process from end to end, initially giving you a general Overview, going then to the specifics of the pre- and post-sales processes, along with guidance on how to secure a deal which will leave you and your potential customer with the good experience for future partnerships. In detail, you will learn how to:

- Generate opportunities to sell your products
- Arrange meetings
- Learn how to prepare your offer for a successful deal
- Build trust
- Handle complaints
- Develop repeat business with your clients
- Be on top of your integrity, learning about business etiquette
- Keep up with your objectives and sales targets

About the Authors

Dr Roberto Castangia has been working for over twenty years as a commercial director and independent consultant in the food, pharmaceutical and biotechnological sectors. His proven experience in multinational and medium-sized enterprises, focuses on commercial growth strategies, business development and successful team building, generating multi-million-dollar sales. As communication expert, he has developed and implemented numerous training programmes, educating dozens of sales teams worldwide. His profound interest in the technical-commercial sector contributes to the success in building companies that drive sustainable growth through people and processes.

Dr Mattia Cassanelli has been working for ten years as a trainer and technical sales consultant in the food, pharmaceutical and biotechnological sectors. The commercial experience combined with a highly specialised scientific background has allowed the development of commercial agreements with over 500 customers all over the world, involving small companies to large corporations. During his career he has supported and trained dozens of professional figures, such as university students, operators in the tourism-hotel sector, freelancers and commercial professionals. The field of interest focuses on technical-scientific aspects and soft skills, with the aim of catalysing professional growth in dynamic and cooperative environments.

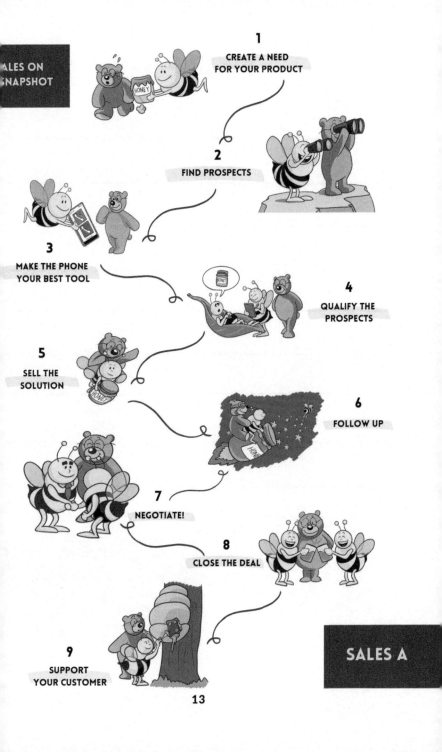

1
CREATE A NEED
FOR YOUR PRODUCT

2
FIND PROSPECTS

3
MAKE THE PHONE
YOUR BEST TOOL

4
QUALIFY THE
PROSPECTS

5
SELL THE
SOLUTION

6
FOLLOW UP

7
NEGOTIATE!

8
CLOSE THE DEAL

9
SUPPORT
YOUR CUSTOMER

SALES A

13

NOTES

CREATE A NEED
FOR YOUR PRODUCT

CREATE A NEED
FOR YOUR PRODUCT

1
MARKET RESEARCH

2
LISTEN

3
DEVELOP YOUR VALUE PROPOSITION*

1. After **researching** for what bees like most, Bonny Bee found that bees **need** honey from the forest.
2. Bonny Bee was told that this special honey is great for bees and bears.
3. Bonny Bee then started selling honey as an energy drink.

Statement that summarises the benefit of a product or service against competitive options

A2

FIND NEW PROSPECTS

FIND NEW PROSPECTS

1
DO MARKETING PROMOTION

2
KEEP LOOKING FOR NEW PROSPECTS*

3
ASK FOR REFERENCES (TO EXISTING ONES)

1. Bonny Bee and Bruno Bear want to sell their special honey to other bees.
2. They **ask around** who would benefit from having their honey.
3. They will approach them and offer their special forest honey.

*An individual who is a potential purchaser of your product or service

18

MAKE THE PHONE YOUR BEST TOOL

MAKE THE PHONE
YOUR BEST TOOL

1
FIND AN EASY WAY TO REACH OUT TO YOUR PROSPECT

2
CALLS ARE ALWAYS PREFERRED TO EMAILS

3
ENGAGE WITH IN-PERSON MEETINGS WHEN YOU CAN

1. Bonny Bee and Bruno Bear arrange a **call for a discussion** about forest honey.
2. They **engage** with bees by talking about common interests too, not just honey.

A4

QUALIFY
THE PROSPECTS

QUALIFY
THE PROSPECTS

1
**PREPARE FOR
YOUR PROSPECT**

2
**GATHER THE
INFORMATION**

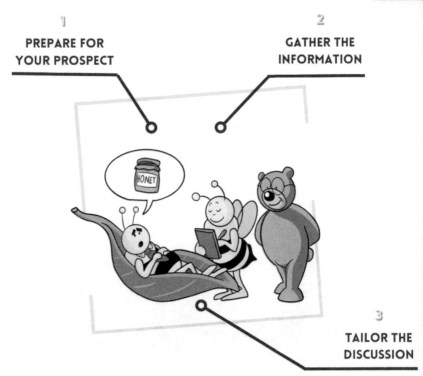

3
**TAILOR THE
DISCUSSION**

1. Bonny Bee and Bruno Bear **examine** bees' **preferences and habits**.
2. They look for details and **information** in **preparation for calls** and meetings.
3. They can then leverage what was studied and **tailor** the **discussion** in their favour.

SELL THE SOLUTION

1

**TRUST YOUR
PRODUCT**

2

**SELL THE VALUE,
NOT THE PRODUCT**

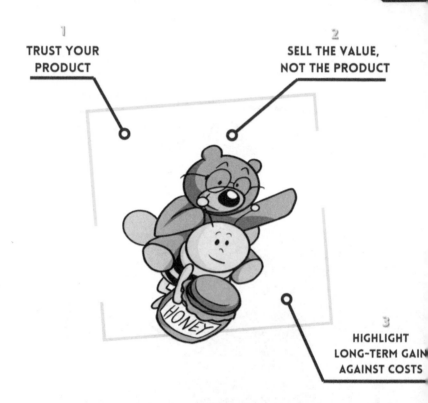

3

**HIGHLIGHT
LONG-TERM GAIN
AGAINST COSTS**

1. To sell honey, Bonny Bee and Bruno Bear need to focus on **why** their honey is **special**.
2. They sell the idea that the honey is great energy. They are not selling just honey.
3. They **list** the **advantages** of their honey when talking with other bees.

FOLLOW UP

1
CHASE YOUR PROSPECT

2
ASK FOR UPDATES

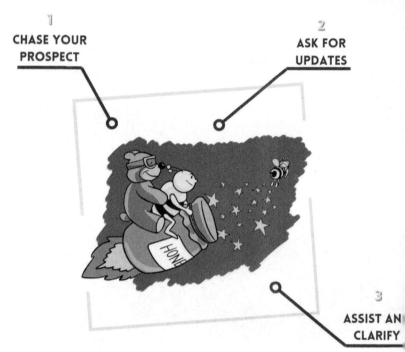

3
ASSIST AN CLARIFY

1. Bonny Bee and Bruno Bear always **keep track** and monitor the bees that show interest in their honey.
2. They always **keep** themselves **up to date**, so they cannot miss the opportunity to sell their honey.
3. They **offer assistance** to bees that are interested in their honey, answering questions and **addressing concerns**.

NEGOTIATE!

1
LEARN TO NEGOTIATE

2
USE NEGOTIATION TACTICS

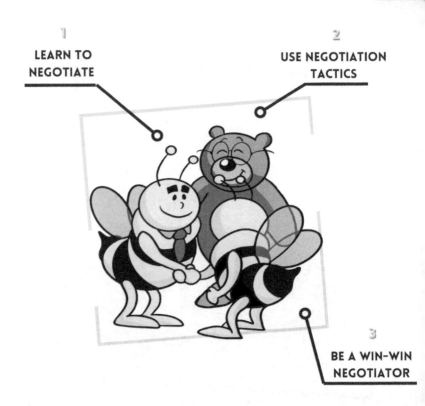

3
BE A WIN-WIN NEGOTIATOR

1. Bonny Bee and Bruno Bear learn how to obtain what they want with **negotiation**.
2. They use several negotiation **tactics** using the SNA*Programme* – *Negotiation*
3. They know that in a sale process, **all parties** should **gain something**.

CLOSE THE DEAL

CLOSE THE DEAL

1 FINALISE THE OUTCOME

2 THANK THE CUSTOMER

3 ALWAYS KEEP YOUR WORD ON PROMISES

1. Bonny Bee and Bruno Bear **always thank** bees for their time and collaboration.
2. They always **offer assistance** to their customers
3. They always **keep** their **promises**.

SUPPORT
YOUR CUSTOMER

SUPPORT
YOUR CUSTOMER

1
MONITOR THE
SATISFACTION OF
YOUR CUSTOMER

2
TREAT YOUR
CUSTOMER AS YOUR
BEST FRIEND

4
ALWAYS BE READY
TO HELP

3
ASK FOR
FEEDBACK

1. After the sale, Bonny Bee and Bruno Bear keep monitoring the bees, ensuring their **satisfaction**.
2. For them it is critical to **build trust** and a genuine relationship.
3. **Feedback** from the bees **is key** for them.
4. If needed, They are **ready to fix problems**.

THE ESSENTIAL OF SALES
PRE-SALES

1
TRUST YOUR PRODUCT

2
SPOT NEW OPPORTUNITIES

3
ACTIVELY BUILD OPPORTUNITIES

4
PASSIVELY BUILD OPPORTUNITIES

5
BUILD A RELATIONSHIP

6
PREPARE YOUR MEETINGS

7
ASK FOR BUDGET CONSTRAINTS (BANT)

8
UNDERSTAND THE AUTHORITY (BANT)

9
UNDERSTAND THE NEED (BANT)

10
ASK FOR TIMELINES (BANT)

SALES B

NOTES

_____

_____

_____

_____

_____

_____

_____

_____

TRUST YOUR PRODUCT

TRUST YOUR PRODUCT

B1

1
KNOW YOUR PRODUCT INSIDE OUT

2
BE PASSIONATE ABOUT YOUR PRODUCT

3
SHARE YOUR PASSION

1. Bonny Bee and Bruno Bear **know all of their product's details** very well.
2. They are very **passionate** about what they sell and love it.
3. They share their **passion** for their honey with other bees.

36

SPOT NEW
OPPORTUNITIES

SPOT NEW OPPORTUNITIES

1
FIND NEW NEEDS TO ADDRESS

2
IDENTIFY THE MARKET

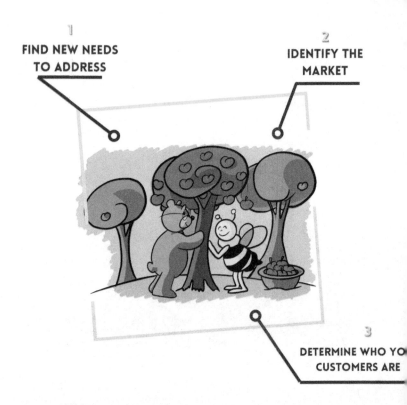

3
DETERMINE WHO YO
CUSTOMERS ARE

1. Bonny Bee and Bruno Bear found that bees that love their honey **also like** apples.
2. They **shake the tree** to collect more apples to sell with their honey.
3. The **new opportunity** shall be related to existing offer **to complement** it.

ACTIVELY
BUILD OPPORTUNITIES

ACTIVELY BUILD OPPORTUNITIES

1
GET IN TOUCH WITH PROSPECTS

2
NETWORK

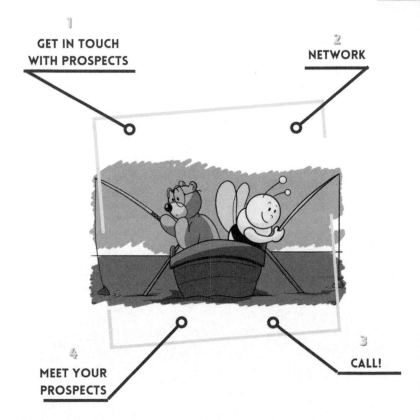

4
MEET YOUR PROSPECTS

3
CALL!

1. Bonny Bee and Bruno Bear fish for **new opportunities**.
2. They develop their **network** by means of **meetings and calls***
3. **In-person** relationships are always **preferred** to emails

*This process is called "Outbound sales"

PASSIVELY
BUILD OPPORTUNITIES

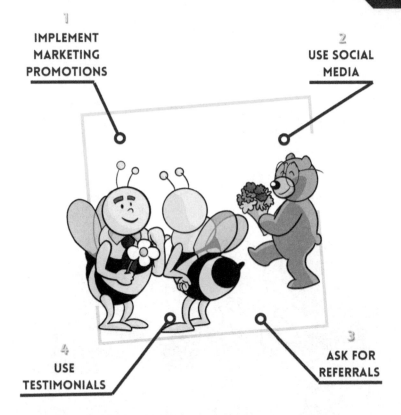

1
IMPLEMENT
MARKETING
PROMOTIONS

2
USE SOCIAL
MEDIA

4
USE
TESTIMONIALS

3
ASK FOR
REFERRALS

1. Bonny Bee and Bruno Bear rely on other bees to **promote** their honey through word of mouth.
2. Other Bees reach out to ask about the honey thanks to the **promotional activity***

This process is called "Inbound sales"

BUILD A RELATIONSHIP

BUILD A
RELATIONSHIP

1
BE FRIENDLY

2
BE HONEST AND TRANSPARENT

3
SHOW INTEGRITY AND BUILD TRUST

1. Bonny Bee and Bruno Bear carefully **water the flower** which will bear the pollen for bees.
2. Likewise, **trust** is built up with other bees based on core values such us **honesty** and **friendship**.

PREPARE YOUR
✦MEETINGS✦

PREPARE YOUR MEETINGS

1
LEARN ABOUT THE
PERSON AND COMPANY

2
UNDERSTAND THE
TOPIC AND NEED

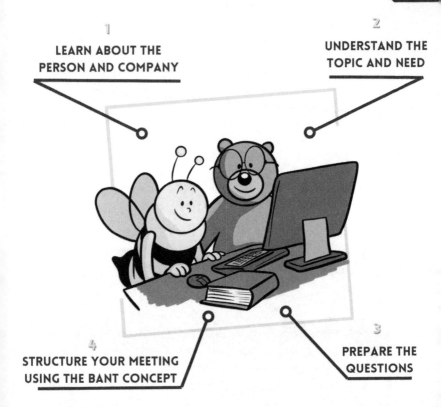

4
STRUCTURE YOUR MEETING
USING THE BANT CONCEPT

3
PREPARE THE
QUESTIONS

- Bonny Bee and Bruno Bear **get prepared** to meet new bees.
- The more **information** is available for the meeting the better.
- **BANT** helps to remember the 4 critical pieces of information for the sales case.

ASK FOR BUDGET
CONSTRAINTS
(BANT)

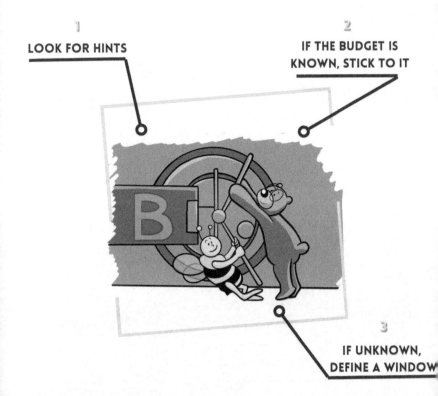

1
LOOK FOR HINTS

2
IF THE BUDGET IS
KNOWN, STICK TO IT

3
IF UNKNOWN,
DEFINE A WINDOW

1. Bonny Bee and Bruno Bear are opening the vault to check what **BUDGET** is available.
2. Having a clear idea about the **value**, enables to tailor the offer against competitors.

UNDERSTAND
THE AUTHORITY
(BANT)

B

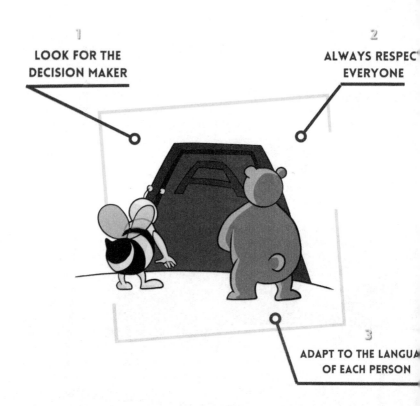

1

**LOOK FOR THE
DECISION MAKER**

2

**ALWAYS RESPEC
EVERYONE**

3

**ADAPT TO THE LANGUA
OF EACH PERSON**

1. Bonny Bee and Bruno Bear **target** the bee **responsible** in the purchase process based on its AUTHORITY.
2. To reach the right one, they have to rely on the **support from others**.
3. Keeping **everyone** highly **valued**, shortcuts the process.

UNDERSTAND THE NEED
(BANT)

UNDERSTAND THE
NEED (BANT)

1
IDENTIFY THE PROBLEM

2
COLLECT REQUIREMENTS

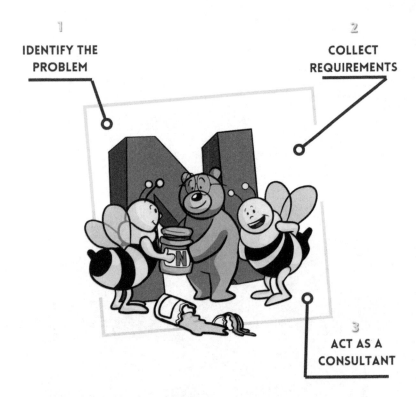

3
ACT AS A CONSULTANT

1. Bonny Bee and Bruno Bear **understand** clearly the **need** of the bee, the honey jar is broken.
2. They propose a **solution** to ensure to **supply** the **demand**.
3. Offering the **solution** to the problem, **outruns** the monetary **concerns**.
4. **Value** is the focus, **not costs**!

52

ASK FOR TIMELINES
(BANT)

ASK FOR TIMELINES
(BANT)

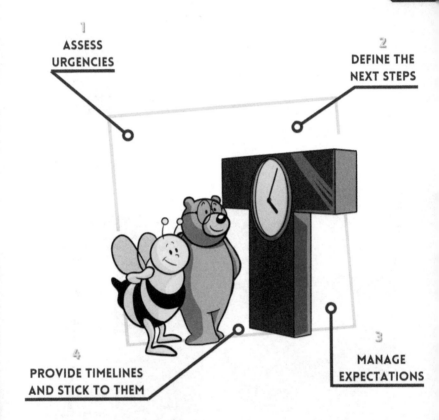

1
ASSESS
URGENCIES

2
DEFINE THE
NEXT STEPS

4
PROVIDE TIMELINES
AND STICK TO THEM

3
MANAGE
EXPECTATIONS

1. Bonny Bee and Bruno Bear **assess** the **turnaround** for delivering their offer.
2. They **promise** only **what can be achieved** while managing **expectations**.
3. **Time** always has a **cost factor**, therefore Bonny Bee and Bruno Bear take the cost of resources into account.

THE ESSENTIAL OF SALES
PRE-SALES

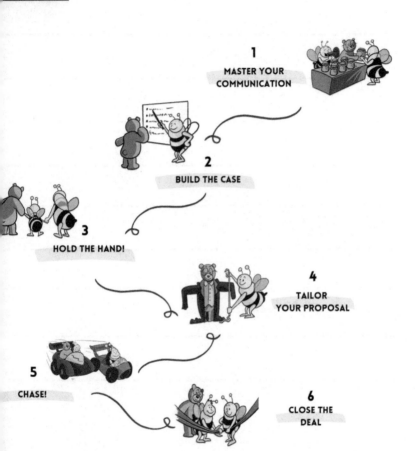

1
MASTER YOUR
COMMUNICATION

2
BUILD THE CASE

3
HOLD THE HAND!

4
TAILOR
YOUR PROPOSAL

5
CHASE!

6
CLOSE THE
DEAL

SALES C

NOTES

MASTER YOUR
COMMUNICATION

MASTER YOUR COMMUNICATION

1
PREPARE YOUR PITCH

2
ADAPT YOUR COMMUNICATION TO YOUR POTENTIAL CLIENT

3
ENGAGE THE POTENTIAL CLIENT IN THE CONVERSATION

1. Bonny Bee and Bruno Bear develop their proposal based on the **strengths and benefits** of their honey.
2. One does not fit all and the **message is adapted** to different requirements.
3. The sale is achieved through **trust** resulting from a more general engagement with client interests and **needs**.

58

BUILD THE CASE

BUILD THE CASE

1
LISTEN ACTIVELY
(80/20 RULE)

2
CONFIRM
REQUIREMENTS

3
MEET
EXPECTATIONS

1. During conversations, Bonny Bee and Bruno Bear spend most of the time as **active listeners** (80%)*
2. Open questions help to gather the full picture
3. **Needs** and **expectations** are outlined and agreed
4. Their talking is limited to **summaries** and **solution propositions** (20%)

*Active listening is the process to understand the message by rephrasing it and ask for confirmation.

HOLD THE HAND!

HOLD THE HAND!

1

**GUIDE THE CUSTOMER
THROUGH THE PROCESS**

2

**WORK THROUG
ANY CONCERN**

3

**REASSURE YOU ME
THE REQUIREMENT**

1. Bonny Bee and Bruno Bear understand the process can be new for the bee and go through the process **together**.
2. When facing concerns they clarify using **examples** and previously addressed cases
3. Requirements are **agreed and delivered** accordingly.

TAILOR YOUR PROPOSAL

TAILOR YOUR PROPOSAL

1
CREATE A BESPOKE SOLUTION

2
BE SPECIFIC AND ACCURATE

3
UPSELL IF/WHEN POSSIBLE

1. Bonny Bee and Bruno Bear **adapt each offer**/proposal to their client.
2. **Clarity** is a must for time, deliverables* and costs.
3. When the main requirements are covered, then include (non-essential) **complementary items**.

*Deliverables refer to the outcome to be provided to the client as part of a sales agreement or contract.

64

CHASE!

CHASE!

C5

1
FOLLOW UP

2
ASK FOR UPDATES

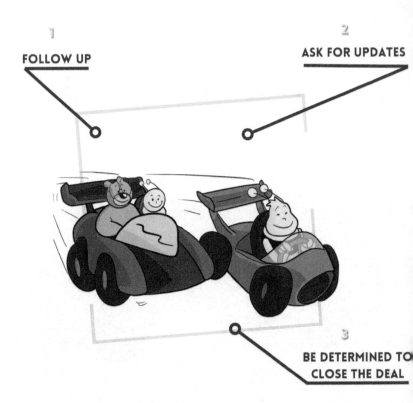

3
BE DETERMINED TO CLOSE THE DEAL

1. Bonny Bee and Bruno Bear **keep close** to the client bee in her decision making process.
2. **Chasing** is always a **compromise** between providing **assistance** for the final decision and **sealing the deal**.

CLOSE THE DEAL

CLOSE THE DEAL

1
MAXIMISE YOUR PROFIT

2
THANK THE CLIE

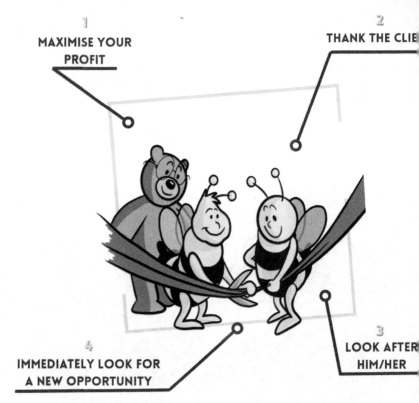

4
IMMEDIATELY LOOK FOR A NEW OPPORTUNITY

3
LOOK AFTER HIM/HER

1. Bonny Bee and Bruno Bear have carefully followed the **sales process** and are now cutting the ribbon for the new partnership.
2. The deal always gives a **benefit** to both the client and the seller.
3. The support for the **after sales** phase begins.
4. There is no time to waste, Bonny Bee and Bruno Bear will now start to build **another case**.

THE ESSENTIAL OF SALES
POST SALE

1

SUPPORT YOUR CUSTOMERS

2

TREAT YOUR CUSTOMER AS YOUR BEST FRIEND

3

CHASE YOUR MONEY

4

ASK FOR REFERRALS

5

ASK FOR FEEDBACK

6

BE PROACTIVE AND MINIMISE COMPLAINTS

7

IF DISRUPTIONS OCCUR, MANAGE THEM!

SALES D

NOTES

SUPPORT
YOUR CUSTOMERS

1 KEEP YOUR WORD!

2 FULFILL THE NEED

3 KEEP EFFICIENT COMMUNICATION

1. Bonny Bee and Bruno Bear **honour** their **word** by making themselves available for **assistance** at any request.
2. **Integrity** on promises will be the **base of trust**.
3. They make sure their **product** gives back what is **expected**.
4. The **communication** is kept **continuous** after the deal just like during the qualification process.

TREAT YOUR CUSTOMER AS YOUR BEST FRIEND

TREAT YOUR CUSTOMER AS YOUR BEST FRIEND

1
ALWAYS BE
AVAILABLE

2
REPLY WITHIN
24 HOURS

3
BE PROFESSIONAL

1. Bonny Bee and Bruno Bear ensure an immediate communication, being supportive for any enquiry.
2. The rapport they develop is based on **trust** and **honesty**.
3. They always balance **personal** with **professional**, **engaging** with the customer **openness**.

74

CHASE YOUR MONEY

CHASE YOUR MONEY

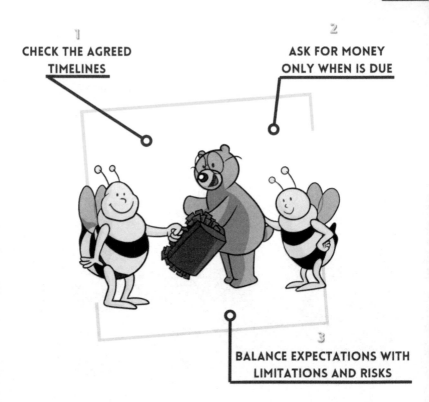

1 CHECK THE AGREED TIMELINES

2 ASK FOR MONEY ONLY WHEN IS DUE

3 BALANCE EXPECTATIONS WITH LIMITATIONS AND RISKS

1. Bonny Bee and Bruno Bear **monitor** the **progress** of their plan ensuring that agreed terms are delivered.
2. Requesting **money** is **part of the deal** as well as deliverables. Asking for it at the **wrong time** however, can lead to **loss of trust**.
3. Bonny Bee and Bruno Bear build trust **advising** on limitations and **risks**.

ASK FOR REFERRALS

ASK FOR REFERRALS

1
IDENTIFY YOUR BEST CUSTOMERS

2
CONTACT YOUR REFERRALS

3
REMEMBER TO REWARD (SEE RECIPROCITY)

1. Bonny Bee and Bruno Bear rely on the **trust** built for additional **promotion**.
2. Asking their close customers to **refer other** who will benefit from the same solution, will ensure the **success** of the product.
3. A **referral is a favour** bound to reciprocity* for which Bonny Bee and Bruno Bear have to **reward back** (free item/discount/extra service).

Reciprocity is a principle of returning a favour to someone who has helped you before.

ASK FOR FEEDBACK

1
QUESTION YOUR PRODUCT PERFORMANCES

2
ASK HOW TO IMPROVE IT

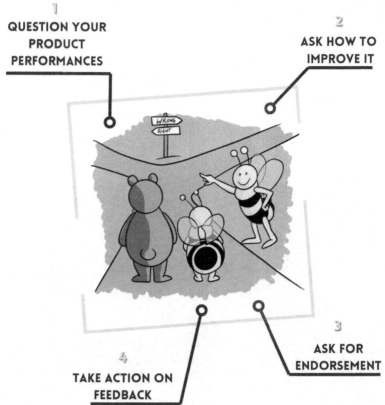

3
ASK FOR ENDORSEMENT

4
TAKE ACTION ON FEEDBACK

1. Bonny Bee and Bruno Bear rely on their (customer) bee to **improve** their offer by asking for **feedback** their **experience**.
2. Having their product **advertised** (endorsed) will support **benefit** recognition.
3. Bonny Bee and Bruno Bear always ensure **feedbacks** is followed by **implementations**.

BE PROACTIVE AND MINIMISE COMPLAINTS

BE PROACTIVE AND
MINIMISE COMPLAINTS

1
RECOGNISE SIGNS
OF CONCERNS

2
RECOGNISE WEAKNESSES
WHEN AND IF NEEDED

4
PUT CORRECTIVE
ACTIONS IN PLACE

3
SOLVE THE PROBLEM
QUICKLY!

1. Product **failures are common**, denying them will destroy trust
2. Bonny Bee and Bruno Bear proactively **address weaknesses** by relying on feedback
3. **Corrective measures** are critical to retain successful products.

IF DISRUPTIONS OCCUR, MANAGE THEM!

IF DISRUPTIONS OCCUR, MANAGE THEM!

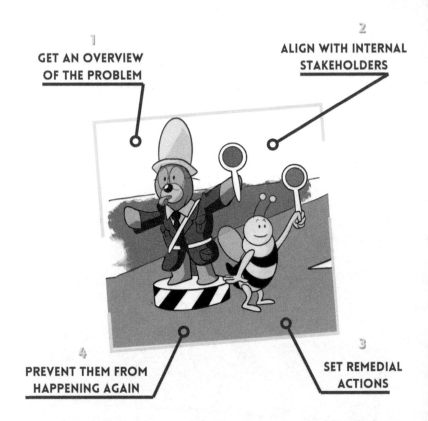

1
GET AN OVERVIEW
OF THE PROBLEM

2
ALIGN WITH INTERNAL
STAKEHOLDERS

4
PREVENT THEM FROM
HAPPENING AGAIN

3
SET REMEDIAL
ACTIONS

1. Bonny Bee and Bruno Bear have identified an **issue** and promptly manage **solutions with actions**.
2. An **improvement process** is put into place to guarantee a resolution and **prevention** for future cases.

ANDLING
MPLAINTS

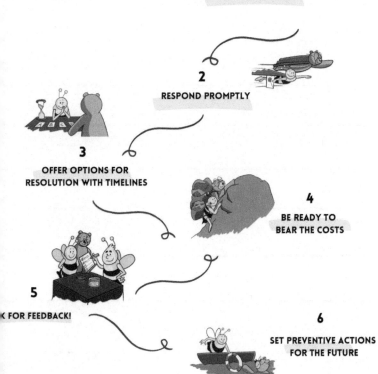

1

EVALUATE COMPLAINT

2

RESPOND PROMPTLY

3

**OFFER OPTIONS FOR
RESOLUTION WITH TIMELINES**

4

**BE READY TO
BEAR THE COSTS**

5

K FOR FEEDBACK!

6

**SET PREVENTIVE ACTIONS
FOR THE FUTURE**

SALES E

NOTES

EVALUATE COMPLAINT

EVALUATE COMPLAINT

1 UNDERSTAND THE ROOT OF THE PROBLEM

2 COLLECT INFORMATION FROM ALL PARTIES

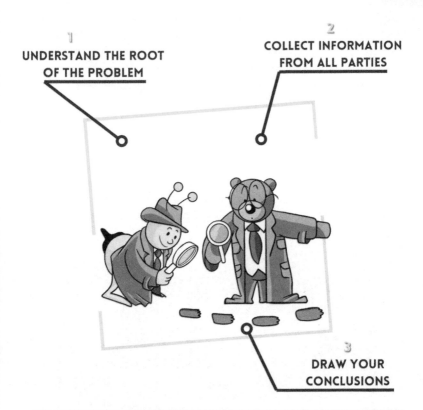

3 DRAW YOUR CONCLUSIONS

1. If a complaint occurs, Bonny Bee and Bruno Bear **listen** to their client **to** fully **understand** the **reasons**.
2. Listening to client's and internal perspectives, **prevents** wrong **assumptions**.
3. With all information gathered, the picture of the complaint becomes clearer.

RESPOND PROMPTLY

1
**MAKE THE MATTER
A HIGH PRIORITY**

2
ACT SWIFTLY

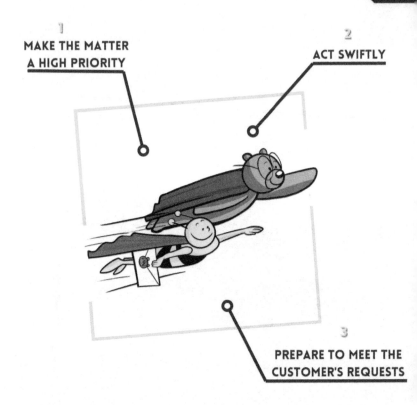

3
**PREPARE TO MEET THE
CUSTOMER'S REQUESTS**

1. Bonny Bee and Bruno Bear **plan** the best **actions** in order to resolve the complaint.
2. Actions are taken on **priority**.
3. **Concessions** may be **needed** to solve the complaint and regain the customer's satisfaction.

OFFER OPTIONS FOR RESOLUTION WITH TIMELINES

OFFER OPTIONS FOR
RESOLUTION WITH TIMELINES

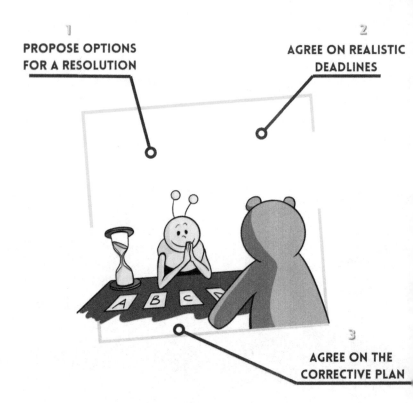

1

**PROPOSE OPTIONS
FOR A RESOLUTION**

2

**AGREE ON REALISTIC
DEADLINES**

3

**AGREE ON THE
CORRECTIVE PLAN**

1. Bonny Bee and Bruno Bear propose
   their plan for **resolution** to the client.
2. The plan contains **deadlines**, so all the
   expectations are **realistic**.
3. At this stage, **clarity** on the agreed
   actions to undertake **is essential**.

BE READY TO ACCEPT THE COSTS

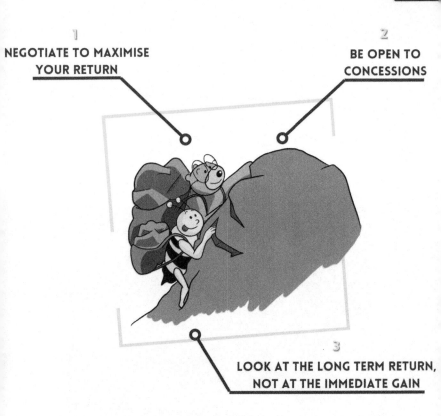

1
NEGOTIATE TO MAXIMISE YOUR RETURN

2
BE OPEN TO CONCESSIONS

3
LOOK AT THE LONG TERM RETURN, NOT AT THE IMMEDIATE GAIN

1. Bonny Bee and Bruno Bear need to find the **compromise** between customer **satisfaction** and **profit**.
2. They make sustainable **adjustments and concessions** aiming for the **long relationship** with the client.
3. A concession today could lead to a much larger **return** in **future**.

ASK FOR FEEDBACK!

ASK FOR FEEDBACK!

1
**CALL TO ASSESS
THE OUTCOME**

2
**ASK HOW TO IMPROVE
YOUR PRODUCTS/SERVICES**

3
**BE OPEN
TO CRITICISM**

1. Bonny Bee and Bruno Bear **check** to see if the complaint is **resolved** or if it persists.
2. For a **continuous improvement**, they ask for feedback.
3. **Criticism** should be seen as an **opportunity** to **implement** the processes and **set corrective actions**.

96

SET PREVENTIVE ACTIONS FOR THE FUTURE

SET PREVENTIVE ACTIONS
FOR THE FUTURE

1

**LEARN THE
LESSONS**

2

**PREVENT THE PROBLEM
IN FUTURE**

3

**KEEP PROACTIVE
(NOT REACTIVE)**

1. Bonny Bee and Bruno Bear have learned the **lesson**, which is **documented** for future reference.
2. Being **proactive** is more important than being **reactive**.
3. **Foresee** customer's **response/feedback** helps minimise complaints and **increase** the overall **satisfaction**.

THE ESSENTIAL OF SALES

1

KNOW YOUR CUSTOMER

2

ASSESS VALUES AND NEEDS

3

KEEP IN TOUCH

4

**DEVELOP
NEW OPPORTUNITIES**

5

**PLAN FOR
THE NEXT PROPOSAL**

SALES F

NOTES

KNOW YOUR CUSTOMER

1

MONITOR CHANGES RELATED
TO THE COMPANY

2

MONITOR CHANGES
RELATED TO ITS MEMBERS

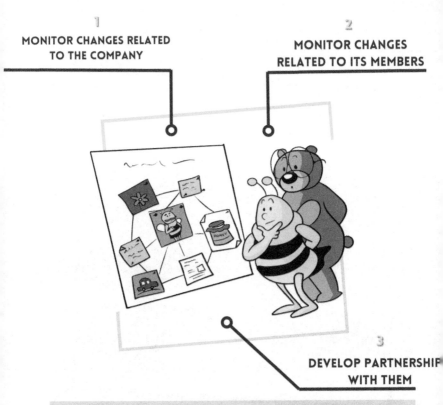

3

DEVELOP PARTNERSHIP
WITH THEM

1. Bonny Bee and Bruno Bear always **check** the **latest** information about their customer and the company in which they work.
2. Changes in **people's role**, could open opportunities elsewhere with **new partnerships**.
3. Changes in the **company** could imply need for **more or new requirements**.

ASSESS VALUES AND NEEDS

ASSESS VALUES AND NEEDS

1
**KEEP YOURSELF
UP TO DATE**

2
**CONDUCT MARKET RESEARCH
AND UNDERSTAND NEW TRENDS**

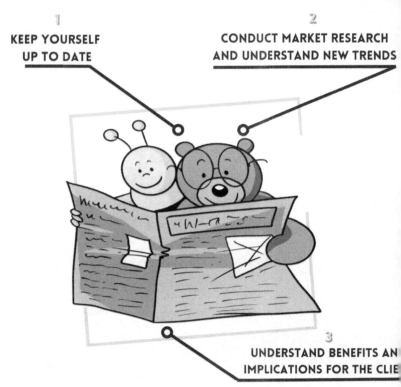

3
**UNDERSTAND BENEFITS AN
IMPLICATIONS FOR THE CLIE**

1. Bonny Bee and Bruno Bear keep themselves **up-to-date** on their **market trends**.
2. When changes occur, the **product** is **adapted** or **new solutions** are **presented** to the client
3. You ought to be **ahead** of you **client**, always!

KEEP IN TOUCH

KEEP IN TOUCH

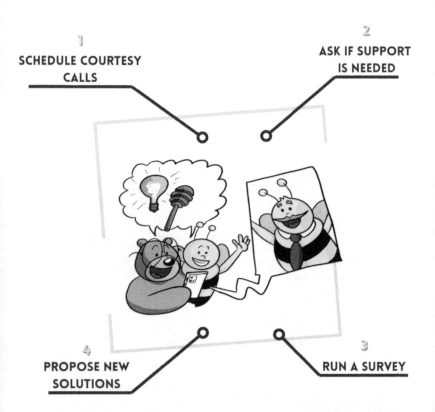

1 SCHEDULE COURTESY CALLS

2 ASK IF SUPPORT IS NEEDED

4 PROPOSE NEW SOLUTIONS

3 RUN A SURVEY

1. Bonny Bee and Bruno Bear are **always in touch** with their clients.
2. **Surveys** are useful to gather the customer's **feedback** and to **develop** the product.
3. **Feedback** from a client could become a **solution** for **another client**.

DEVELOP NEW OPPORTUNITIES

1
EVALUATE NEW INFORMATION

2
REALIGN NEEDS WITH NEW PROPOSALS

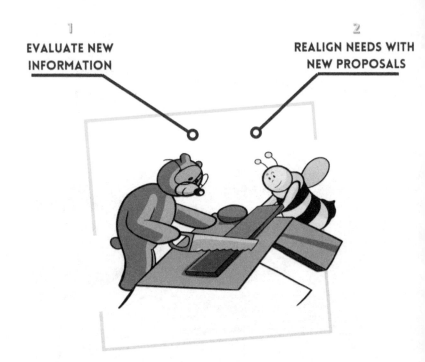

1. Bonny Bee and Bruno Bear **check** the **new information** provided by the client.
2. Discussing **general aspects** of the ongoing project helps develop **new opportunities** with the **same client**.

PLAN FOR THE NEXT PROPOSAL

PLAN FOR THE NEXT PROPOSAL

1
**PROPOSE THE
NEW SOLUTION**

2
**REVIEW IT WITH
THE CLIENT**

3
**CLOSE THE
NEW DEAL**

1. Bonny Bee and Bruno Bear propose a
   new plan to the client based on the
   information gathered.
2. This is **reviewed together**, making
   sure that the client is happy and ready
   to continue the **collaboration**.

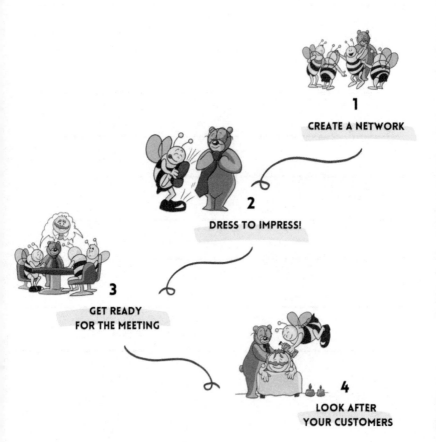

1

CREATE A NETWORK

2

DRESS TO IMPRESS!

3

**GET READY
FOR THE MEETING**

4

**LOOK AFTER
YOUR CUSTOMERS**

SALES G

NOTES

CREATE A NETWORK

CREATE A NETWORK

1
ORGANISATION AND PREPARATION IS KEY TO MEET PEOPLE OF INTEREST

2
EXCHANGE KNOWLEDGE AND CONTACTS

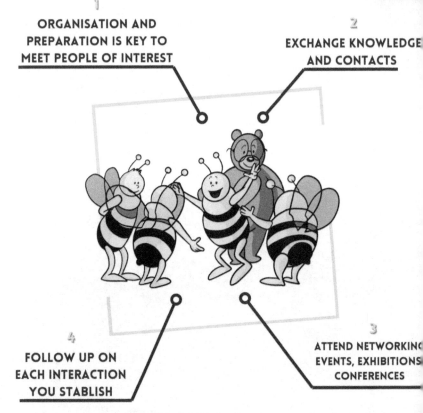

4
FOLLOW UP ON EACH INTERACTION YOU STABLISH

3
ATTEND NETWORKING EVENTS, EXHIBITIONS CONFERENCES

1. Bonny Bee and Bruno Bear keep **developing** their **network**. This is a mixture of clients, collaborators and people with the same interest.
2. Their network is **expanded** through meetings, calls and events.
3. It is important to keep a **continuous communication** with the network.

114

DRESS TO IMPRESS!

DRESS TO IMPRESS!

1
DRESS
APPROPRIATELY

2
BE POLITE

3
KEEP POISE
AT ALL TIMES

4
BE PROFESSIONAL

1. When meeting clients, Bonny Bee and Bruno Bear check their **image** and **appearance** a priority.
2. They are **respectful**, **kind** and **considerate**.
3. In high-pressure situations, they **keep** their **cool**.
4. **Politeness** and **professionalism** are a must always.

GET READY FOR THE MEETING

1
PICK THE RIGHT LOCATION
(OFFICE/CAFÉ/RESTAURANT)

2
PREPARE THE MEETING WITH
AGENDA AND EXPECTATIONS

4
REMAIN TIMELY FROM
START TO FINISH

3
NOTE KEY POINTS AND
FOLLOW UP ACTIONS

1. Bonny Bee and Bruno Bear **plan** and **schedule** their meeting in the most efficient way. This means a **suitable location**, free of noise and distractions.
2. The meeting needs to have a **structure** to follow (agenda) and **objectives** to achieve.
3. **Minutes** of the meeting are recorded and used for follow up actions.

LOOK AFTER YOUR CUSTOMERS

1. ENGAGE!
2. ENTERTAIN!
3. ENJOY!

1. During meetings, Bonny Bee and Bruno Bear remember the **3E's rule**.
2. **Build rapport** though discussing common interests, upcoming events, compliments on projects and accomplishments
3. **Avoid** topics such as politics, sex, illness or diet, weather and unless you know well someone, family and marital status.

1

ANTICIPATE RISKS AND SUCCESS

2

TRACK YOUR PROGRESS

3

DELIVER!

SALES H

NOTES

_____

_____

_____

_____

_____

_____

_____

_____

_____

ANTICIPATE RISKS AND SUCCESS

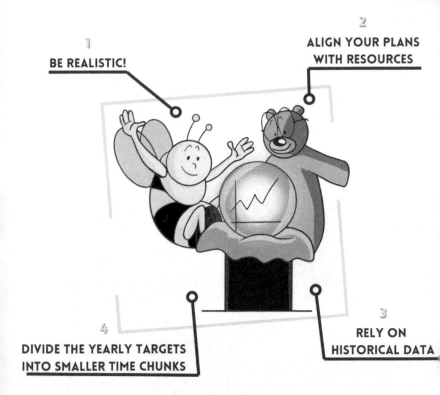

1
BE REALISTIC!

2
ALIGN YOUR PLANS
WITH RESOURCES

4
DIVIDE THE YEARLY TARGETS
INTO SMALLER TIME CHUNKS

3
RELY ON
HISTORICAL DATA

1. Bonny Bee and Bruno Bear are **looking ahead** to define their objectives
2. Forecasts must be **realistic** and supported by available **resources**.
3. **Historical data** can help the **accuracy** of the forecast.
4. **Big targets** are easier to achieve if **broken down further** into monthly, weekly and daily sales objectives.

TRACK YOUR PROGRESS

TRACK YOUR PROGRESS

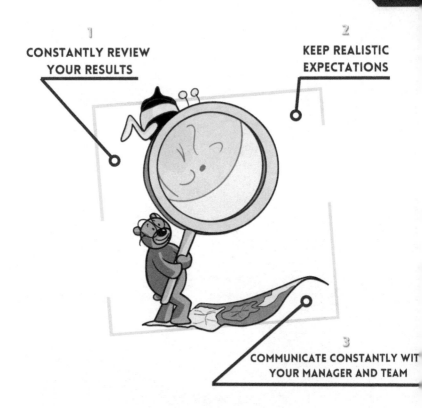

1
CONSTANTLY REVIEW YOUR RESULTS

2
KEEP REALISTIC EXPECTATIONS

3
COMMUNICATE CONSTANTLY WITH YOUR MANAGER AND TEAM

1. Bonny Bee and Bruno Bear **constantly check** the **actual** sales against the **forecast*** and use it as a guideline.
2. **Key Performance Indicators** (KPI) help **measure** sales results.
3. **Communication** within the team is **fundamental** to prevent falling behind targets.

*Forecast refers to a prediction or estimate of future sales performance, typically within a specified time frame

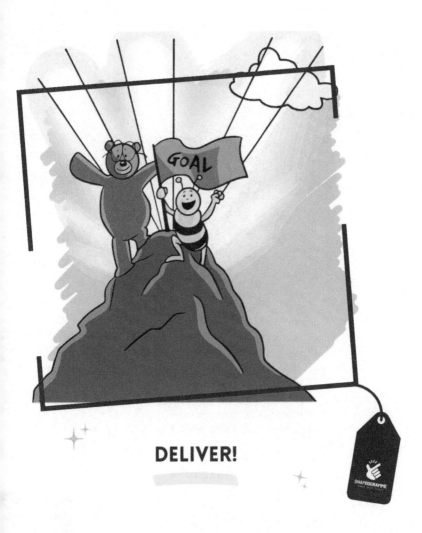

DELIVER!

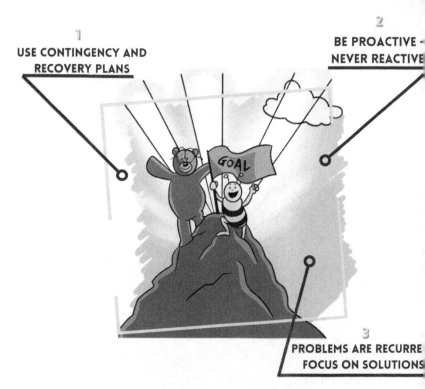

1
USE CONTINGENCY AND
RECOVERY PLANS

2
BE PROACTIVE –
NEVER REACTIVE

3
PROBLEMS ARE RECURRE
FOCUS ON SOLUTIONS

1. Bonny Bee and Bruno Bear always have a
   contingency and **recovery plan** to out into
   action in case the forecast is not met.
2. Bonny Bee and Bruno Bear are **proactive**
   and focus on **solutions** as soon as they see
   a problem on the horizon.
3. The **goal** is **achieved** as a result of **vision**,
   commitment and **determination**.

DON'T MISS
THE NEXT BOOK
IN THE SERIES!

**LEARN MORE ABOUT OUR BOOKS AND SERVICES ON
WWW.SNAPROGRAMME.COM**

Printed in Great Britain
by Amazon

37204067R00076